Aa
Bb
Cc
Dd
Ee
Ff
Gg
Hh
Ii
Jj
Kk
Ll
Mm
Nn
Oo
Pp
Qq
Rr
Ss
Tt
Uu
Vv
Ww
Xx
Yy
Zz

Zip

Zip is a friendly space alien from planet Zee. He loves to learn. Zip uses his hands to speak to his friends. He can't wait to teach the people of planet Earth all about sign language. Zip is the captain of his spaceship.

Pella

Pella is Zip's best friend. She also comes from planet Zee. Pella is very brave. Although she is a little younger than Zip and Statz, she isn't afraid of anything and is always the first of the three friends to try new things.

Statz

Statz is in charge of computers on the spaceship. He loves gadgets. Statz uses his Zablet to help him and his friends out of sticky situations. He is excited to learn about planet Earth and all the people who live here.

Goober

Goober is an unexpected guest on the friends' adventures. A greedy and naughty space stowaway, Goober has the ability to change his colour and shape so is always jumping out and surprising Zip, Pella and Statz.

Zip's top tips

Zip and friends are here to help you talk in a fun new way - spell with your fingers and talk with your hands. Follow these top tips to get the most from their adventures:

- **Share the book together and enjoy the story**
- **Play with the signs**
- **Use Zip's alphabet to make your own words**
- **Visit Space School, enjoy the activities and have fun**
- **Watch out for Goober...**

SignSpell
Zip and the Animal Adventure

The spaceship has landed in a field full of sheep.
Zip, Pella and Statz are off to explore the local wildlife.

They can't wait to see the animals of planet Earth up close.

Zip thinks it will be just like going on safari.

Sheep

Animals

The three friends love animals.

On planet Zee, Pella's favourite animal is the zyloplop. They are purple and yellow, and very soft and loving. Pella likes the cuddles they give and the way they wobble when they walk.

Zip and Statz like zyloplops too, but they don't like being licked by zyloplops' big sloppy tongues. Yuck!

The three friends set out on their animal adventure. Zip has taken his binoculars out of his backpack and Statz is ready to take photographs on his Zablet.

"I wonder which animals we will see," says Zip.

"Look," says Pella, "there's something flapping in that tree. What is it, Statz?"

Statz looks up the animal on his Zablet.
"It's a bird," he says, "and it's blue just like me!"

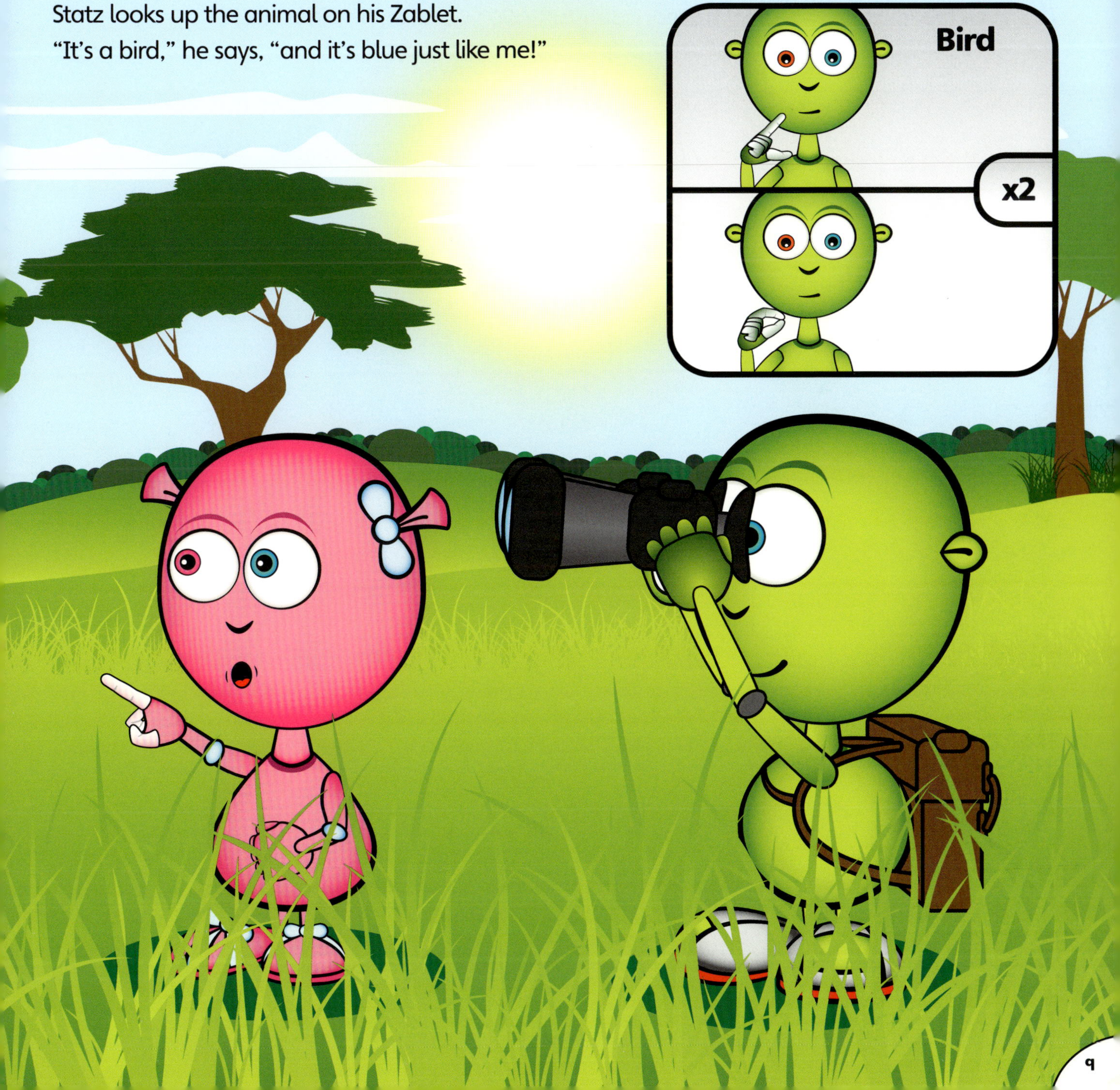

Zip, Pella and Statz want to see more animals after spotting the bird. They walk through the trees until they get to some tall green grass. It swishes around in the gentle breeze.

"We could easily get lost in this grass!" says Zip.

When the three friends reach the end of the tall grass they see a furry animal running in circles with its tongue hanging out.

“What’s that animal doing?” asks Zip.

“That’s a dog,” says Statz, “I think it’s chasing its tail.”

“What a silly thing to do,” says Zip. “I think it looks fun!” laughs Pella.

Dog

Zip, Pella and Statz are excited when they see two more animals.

“That little grey animal is a mouse,” says Statz, “and that animal hiding behind the tree is a cat.”

“The cat looks like it wants to eat the mouse,” says Zip.

Pella is happy when the mouse hides in a hollow log out of the cat’s way.
“I hope the mouse doesn’t become the cat’s dinner,” she says.

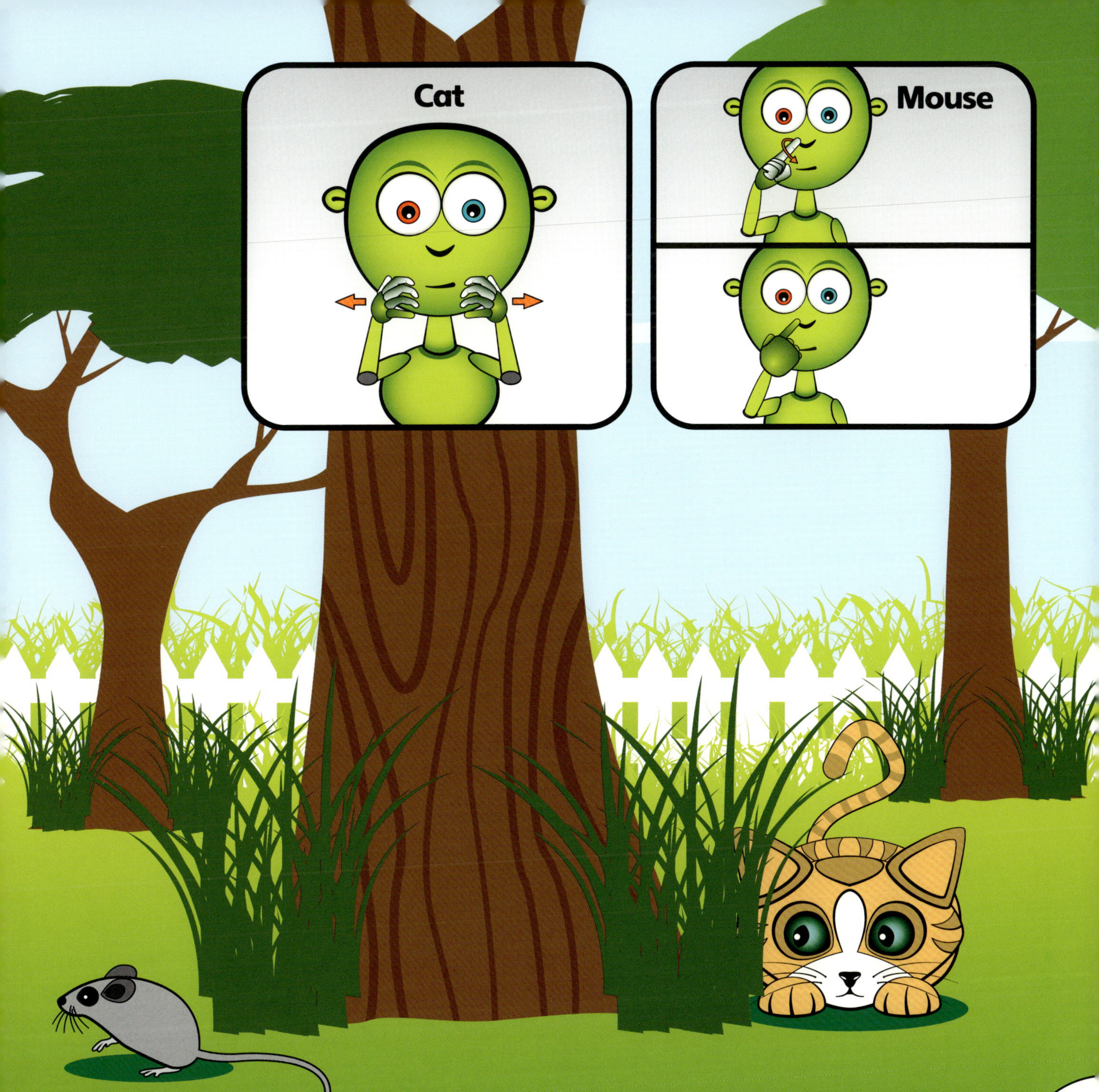
Cat
Mouse

Space School

Here are some animals from Statz's photograph album.
See if you can spell each one using Zip's alphabet.

Zip tries to stop Pella thinking about the greedy cat chasing the poor mouse. "Let's play a game," he says.

Zip goes to get his ball. As he opens his backpack a big fly buzzes out, making him jump. How did that get in there?

Fly

Zip, Pella and Statz start playing with the ball in the field. The ball bounces away from Pella and rolls to a stop in the hollow log where the mouse is hiding. The mouse runs out of the log and the cat chases after it.

“Oh no!” says Pella.

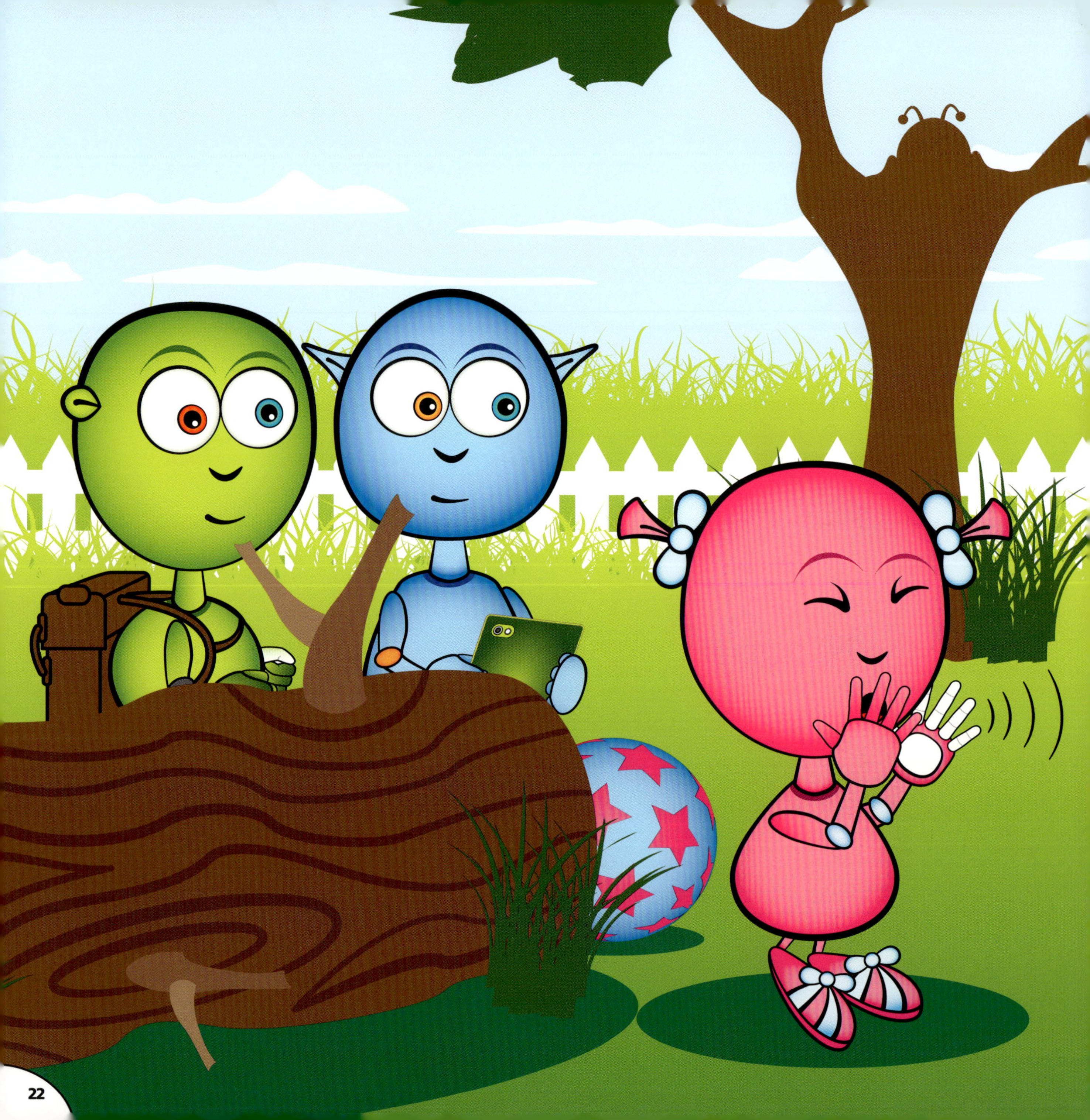

The cat chases the mouse around the field.
It's getting close enough to catch it.
"Stop!" shouts Pella.

The cat is so scared that it stops in its tracks.
The mouse runs off and hides behind a tree.

"Phew!" says Pella.

Zip carries on playing with the ball. He sees a tree and aims the ball at its trunk.

"Be careful, Zip," says Statz. "Don't scare the animals." His warning is too late.

Zip has kicked the ball too hard. It bounces all around the field. It hits a tree and lands in between a horse and a cow, making them run away.

Horse
Cow

Space School

Take a look at the animals below; you may have seen them in the story.
See if you can remember how to sign them.

Sheep

Horse

Cow

Fly

Animals

Dog

It's getting dark and is time to leave, so Zip starts to put his things away. A little worm wiggles next to his backpack.

"That's strange," says Zip, "I only had one ball, but now I have two." He reaches into his backpack to grab the new ball.

"Careful," says Pella, "that's not a ball."

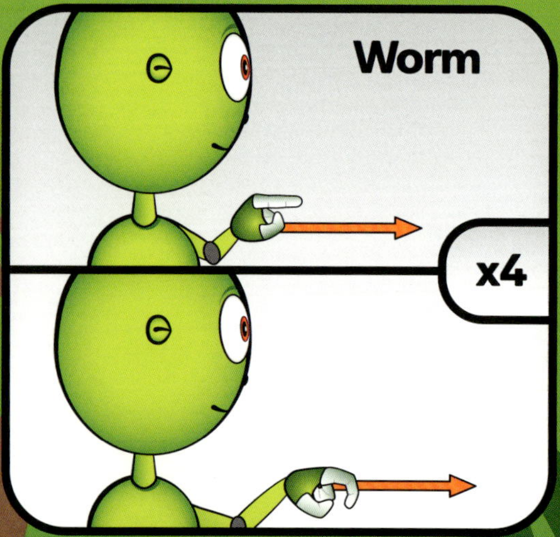

GOOBER!

Zip's Signs

Fun things to do

Now that you have read all about Zip and the Animal Adventure, here are some fun things for you to do:

- **Create your own animal adventure photo album - draw, make or cut out photographs from magazines**
- **If you were on an animal adventure on planet Zee, what animals would you see?**
- **Why do dogs chase their tails?**
- **How would you feel if you saw a cat chasing a mouse?**
- **How would you look after a zyloplop?**
- **Teach a friend the signs for some animals you see everyday**

First published 2013 by Signature

SignSpell® stories created by Signature
Designed and illustrated by Igloo Imaging Ltd.